Mysterious Cheshire

by

Philip Rickman

DALESMAN BOOKS
1980

THE DALESMAN PUBLISHING COMPANY LTD.
CLAPHAM (via Lancaster), NORTH YORKSHIRE

First published 1980

© Philip Rickman 1980

ISBN: 0 85206 618 X

Uniform with this volume:

MYSTERIOUS DERBYSHIRE
(by Philip Rickman and Graham Nown)

Printed in Great Britain by
GEORGE TODD & SON
Marlborough Street, Whitehaven

CONTENTS

Foreword 5

I   An Enigmatic Grin 7

II   Close to the Edge 9

III   Power Points 14

IV   Going Straight 17

V   Elf Paths 30

VI   The Meddler and the Stones 42

VII   Primitive Cheshire 49

VIII   Natural Magic 53

Appendix i   Small, Dark and Dangerous 60

Appendix ii   Tuning In 60

Bibliography 62

Photographs in the text are on pages 33–40.

FOREWORD

THE Cheshire with which this book deals does not always conform to political boundaries, present or past. It crosses sometimes into Merseyside and takes in areas of what has become Greater Manchester. It also includes much of the city of Manchester, which tends to have stronger ties, both cultural and physical, with Cheshire than with Lancashire, which was covered by an earlier book in this series.

The plans illustrating alignments of ancient sites are not strictly to scale but do correspond more or less to the 1:50,000 O.S. maps, to which readers are referred for more detailed study.

Thanks are due to Joan Rogers for witchlore; Graham Nown for information on Celtic traditions; John Condliffe, editor of the Congleton Chronicle, for the tale of the meddler and the stones; Alan Garner for permission to quote from his radio broadcast on childhood experiences at Alderley Edge; and my wife Carol for checking the text.

"Would you tell me, please, which way I ought to go from here?"

"That depends a good deal on where you want to get to," said the cat.

— **Lewis Carroll,**
Alice in Wonderland.

I

AN ENIGMATIC GRIN

THE Cheshire Cat, it is claimed, goes back much further than Alice in Wonderland. Some assert that the cat is really a domesticated descendant of the Cheshire Wolf, seen grinning from the coat of arms of the eleventh century Earl of Chester. But it was Lewis Carroll, alias the Rev. Charles Dodgson, clergyman and mathematician of Daresbury, who projected the most memorable image of the enigmatic moggie. What Carroll's cat lacks in ferocity it makes up for in subtlety. When the face and the body have vanished the grin remains. But the grin says nothing; merely hints.

Such is the smile on the face of Mysterious Cheshire.

*   *   *   *

Wedged between the marches and the Midlands, the Peaks and the Potteries, Cheshire, like the cat, is superficially bland. Its climate is temperate; it wears its towns and villages comfortably in the folds of its softly-textured landscape. It maintains both decent roads and a decent display of verdant pasture between communities. It breathes evenly.

It is easy to disappear in Cheshire but not easy to get lost. The county has clearly-defined landmarks: Mow Cop with its folly tower in the south, the western hills of Helsby and Overton, the castles Beeston and Peckforton, old and newish, frowning at each other across the valley. And to the north, Alderley Edge and the familiar bowl of Jodrell Bank's radio telescope, a piece of cosmic crockery on the patchwork table cloth of the plain. But if the image of the Cheshire Cat conceals some primeval wolf, then Cheshire's blandness is similarly deceptive. The countryside, like many of the people, seems somehow more reserved than in neighbouring counties. It has its secrets, and to those who suspect those secrets, Cheshire becomes an increasingly subtle county; a place of layers.

The aim of the short series of books to which this one belongs has been to explore man's inner links with a particular area, to trace them back through recorded history and beyond. For beyond history lie the sub-strata of legend and folklore, custom and tradition: stories and patterns of behaviour for which we cannot adequately account—but less fanciful or nebulous than orthodox historians generally consider. What might now be seen as romantic or purely aesthetic reactions to the moods of nature may conceal a highly practical mechanism in which man and the elements are compatible cogs. The turning of the seasons, the cycle of the country calendar, the sacred paths marked out both physically and metaphysically on a knowing landscape.

Every county in Britain, no matter how industrialised or suburbanised, has its old mysterious places. Some are obvious: ancient shrines, Celtic crosses, Stone and Bronze Age monuments, haunted hills and healing wells. Others are more elusive: places of no recorded historical significance that reach out to the imagination via some hazy memory, legend or tradition belonging to no particular era.

Stab scientifically at these timeless spots and their power backs off. Scrutinize them too hard and the magical aura fades away until only the tantalising grin remains. Approach them gently from different angles, viewing them with sidelong glances, evaluating them in the light of their influence on man's emotions and you may still pick up the vibrations of an ancient energy.

But any tour of unknown terrain demands a guide. And who more suited to lead the way through the forgotten pathways of a mysterious Cheshire than that benign guardian of the hollow hill . . . the Wizard of Alderley.

II
CLOSE TO THE EDGE

THERE is nothing archaic or mysterious about Wilmslow. The town is cool, clean, modern, middle-class and carefully detached from the blackened city whence came its wealth. But Wilmslow is the first gateway to Mysterious Cheshire because, at some point in its suburban straggle, it fades imperceptibly into Alderley Edge.

On the surface there's nothing mysterious about Alderley either. It used to have the less-evocative name of Chorley. But there is already one of those in Lancashire. Alderley Edge is not only more distinctive, it allows the town to creep within the ambience of the Edge itself. And the Edge is a world away from Wilmslow.

Although the shops are sprinkled with references to the curiosities of the area, Alderley is no tourist town. And when you begin to climb out of the main street it becomes at first reticent and then almost forbidding. The tall chimneys of the town's richest dwellings rear above the guardian trees and nobody seems to know all the folk who live on the hill. . . .

Alderley is Cheshire's mystical stronghold. Probe a little into the darkened recesses of Britain's occult sub-culture and you find names and addresses from around the Edge occurring with more than coincidental frequency. The esoteric traditions have deep roots in these parts. A 'sane, calm girl' told a man from the Manchester Evening News that, at a Hallowe'en party at Alderley, she had seen a man change into a goat. 'A real goat,' the girl emphasised. 'His face suddenly went all hairy and his head sprouted horns. His eyes turned yellow. It was terrifying.' Doubtless—and not the only transformation of its kind said to have been staged behind the Hammer Film facades of the houses of some of those well-heeled hill-dwellers. But outside, beyond the high walls and hedges, the hill itself nurtures a hopefully more natural magic.

Alderley Edge is where plain meets Pennine on a 600-foot cliff face, bearded with bracken and stubbly trees. The tip of the hill is in the care of the National Trust. Behind and around, the landscape relaxes into coppiced, humped and hollowed fields with a tracery of winding roads and a few scattered farms. The best-known building here, quite close to the Edge, is the pub. It is called The Wizard after the central character in Cheshire's most famous legend.

*   *   *   *

A farmer from Mobberley is taking his finest white mare to sell at Macclesfield Fair when, upon Alderley Edge, he is waylaid by an

9

elderly figure in monkish robes. The old man offers to buy the horse. The farmer, anticipating a better deal in Macclesfield, declines. Whereupon the wizard (for it is he) informs the farmer that he will do no other business this day.

The prediction proves accurate. The farmer, returning disgruntled in the evening, still leading his white mare, encounters the wizard again. This time he is more susceptible to a little bargaining — especially when the wizard, beckoning the farmer to follow him, enters through a pair of huge iron gates into the heart of the hill. Here he reveals a huge cave where a host of armed men lie sleeping, their horses beside them. They will arise again, ready for action, says the wizard, at a time when England faces its greatest crisis.

> *Thrice England shall be lost, thrice won,*
> *Twixt dawn of day and setting sun*
> *Then dabbled wings shall ravens toss*
> *Croaking o'er bloodstained Headless Cross.*

But this prediction is only marginally relevant to the business in hand. The wizard explains that the sleeping warriors are one horse short and, in exchange for the white mare, presents the farmer with liberal quantities of gold and jewels. Returning to the real world the man finds the gates and the old man have disappeared. Subsequent searches prove fruitless, and have done to this day when afternoon picnickers are oft to be found vainly tapping rocks in search of magic doorways.

*   *   *   *

The legend, like most legends, is fixed in no special time scale. Jacqueline Simpson says in *The Folklore of the Welsh Border:* 'This tale has been current in Cheshire since the middle of the eighteenth century and is probably far older; it used to be told by the Rev. Shrigley, the curate of Alderley in 1753, who declared that the events had actually happened some eighty years before his time.' Other sources put the legend several hundred years behind the Rev. Shrigley. Wizards themselves apparently exist outside of space and time, and wizard-spotters occasionally spread rumours of fresh sightings of the old man — if not the iron gates. One alleged manifestation was recorded in a local paper in 1974. The story, as told in local tap-rooms, had it that a robed and bearded figure had been spotted on a path below the Edge. However, robed figures are not exactly unknown in present-day Alderley and sceptics swiftly suggested the apparition was probably the modern magus, Alex Sanders, King of the Witches, a man with an impressive collection of ceremonial regalia and a record of arcane practices around the Edge.

But more of him later. At this point it is perhaps worth studying the nature of the legend of Alderley to see what light it throws on the figure of the Wizard. For instance, one interpretation sees the old man as Merlin and the sleeping warriors as King Arthur and his knights. And it is true that the structure of the legend is repeated throughout Britain, more often than not in Arthurian context. Merlin lies in a cave beneath Bardsey Island, off the Lleyn, North Wales and below Martin Mere, a former lake in West Lancashire. Arthur and his men sleep in hills in Northumbria and Southern Scotland. At Caerleon-on-Usk, in Gwent, the Alderley situation is almost paralleled, with a mortal following a wizard into a cavern where Arthur's knights, fully armoured, await in uneasy slumber the call to arms. Elsewhere the legendary king sleeps beneath the sea, in hollow hills, below medieval castles and within prehistoric monuments. The force is there to be awakened, the legend says; Merlin has the knowledge to accomplish this. But he needs a certain human assistance, symbolised by the changeover of the white horse from mortal to supernatural ownership. Without this mortal mediator the alchemical process can never be complete.

Nevertheless, as Jacqueline Simpson points out, 'The ever-growing fame of Arthur tends to infiltrate into what were originally independent legends; fortunately the wizard of Alderley Edge has so far preserved his individuality and refuses to merge wholly into Merlin.'

The pub sign carries an artist's impression of the wizard, above a lantern. This picture, as with most other representations of the old sorcerer, has a distinct similarity to the image of the Hermit in the

The Hermit — as featured in the Tarot.

Tarot pack. According to ancient lore, the hermit, a bearded, lonely figure, shows the way to an inner knowledge which he has himself attained. His staff is a magic wand, his lamp burns the light of experience and of guidance. He is saying, according to the Tarot interpreter Arthur Edward Waite: 'Where I am, you also may be.' The message from the wizard of Alderley is perhaps much the same.

Whether or not the wizard lives on, his magic remains. It is a belief of the witch covens, who still meet in the area, that Alderley Edge has been the scene of ritual worship since the Bronze Age. Certainly it has been well known to man since those days. It was an ancient centre of copper mining and is still something of a warren. Nearby are Bronze Age burial mounds and somewhere close to the Edge, it is said, is a place of particular sanctity, perhaps once the site of a ritual stone circle. There is also a beacon point, probably known as such long before the threat of a Spanish armada, at a time when fires were lit on certain hill tops as a religious observance. And there is a holy well and a carving on the rocks of a familiar face above a small stone trough of spring water with an invitation to drink where 'the water falls by the Wizard's Will.' Alderley Edge has in abundance that elusive atmosphere known as power of place.

Alan Garner, the Cheshire children's author and playwright, has apparently caught the ancient echoes of Alderley since his own childhood. His early work *The Wierdstone of Brisingamen* chronicles the adventures of a young brother and sister who meet the wizard and become involved in his endless battle against the forces of darkness, personified as elemental giants and squalid gnomes. Garner's story is a strange Cheshire odyssey, evoking the image of a neighbouring ethereal countryside only slightly beyond human perception, somewhere penetrable through the mists of twilight, 'beyond the fields we know,' as the Victorian fantasist Lord Dunsany located it. Sometimes a kind of childish innocence can unbar the gates of these phantom pastures. And in a radio broadcast on 'The Landscape of Childhood,' Garner recalled how, as a boy immobilised by a series of illnesses, he learned to project himself into inner landscapes which became more real to him than his bedfast physical existence. Later, on the Edge, behind his home, he would slide into the same timeless states while contemplating the myriad-coloured strata of the magical cliff. The results were dramatic:

> 'The experience didn't occur often, but sometimes it happened that I had become so engrossed in an aspect of the hill that I unwittingly switched myself off. And on that hill the universe opened. I was shown a totality of space and time; a kaleidoscope of images expanded so quickly that they fragmented. There were too many, too fast, for individual detail or remembrance. They dropped below the subliminal threshold, but I felt the riptide of their surge. . . .'

Garner's technique apparently involved by-passing his own personality, focusing his consciousness on an exterior object and finally connecting with something beyond them both. The ability to do this, it is said, is an essential attribute of the true artist. In *The Occult,* Colin Wilson discusses the projection methods of William Wordsworth and John Cowper Powys, who 'deliberately set out to cultivate "multi-mindedness",' to 'pass out of his own identity into that of people or objects.' Do some places enable this to happen more swiftly, easily and to greater effect than others? Certainly there are other stories exalting Alderley Edge as a place that prompts heightened awareness — a psychic mediator between past, present and future.

There appears to be some kind of time-warp, a converging of images from separate eras, according to Mrs Joan Rogers, a hereditary witch from Denton, Manchester. The witches, she says, know a certain place, an area of the Edge already steeped in ritual, where some trans-dimensional veil is gossamer-thin. 'We have taken different people — not in the Craft — up there and asked them to tell us what comes into their minds. Frequently they have picked up the same things we have picked up.' A popular image, Mrs. Rogers says, is of a figure in 'Joan of Arc type battledress.' At this place too, she says, nature spirits — fairies to some — flit across the vision of those whose perceptions are expanded by the atmosphere of the spot. Like draws like. Pilgrims are pulled to Alderley as to a psychic spa. There is a fount of energy here, accessible through the generating power of ritual or an individual connection with 'the source.'

But beside the positive healing or purifying power is a negative force — debilitating, energy-sapping. Black magicians (not unknown in these parts, as we have seen) might use it to weaken their victims. A psychic sewer runs below the positive power point in the same way that evil spirits are said to congregate just beyond the perimeter of a church. Says Mrs Rogers: 'You can feel it taking away your energy. As if something is pouring energy through you like water; seeping out through your feet until you feel weary and depressed. I have been there with other people and in some cases their hair has actually stood on end. They are like children in their eagerness to get away from the place . . . pulling at you, tugging at your hand. It seems to bring up a primitive fear.'

And then there are the manifestations. No shining Joan of Arc image here. Instead, bad spirits, brown scaly entities, creatures of the mire — the Svart-alfar of Alan Garner's story. Things to pinch the underside of the imagination when the dusk closes over the fields close to the Edge.

III

POWER POINTS

THERE is more to magic circles than you can learn from fairy tales. But the basis is the same. Although they can't all be marked out by toadstools or up-ended stones or sprigs of garlic, magic circles seem to have one thing in common—they all operate as force fields. What happens inside the circle doesn't answer to the same laws as what happens outside. And when you step over the circumference you ought to notice the difference.

The witches talk of a large-scale magic circle in North-East Cheshire. Places roughly on its circumference include Duckinfield, Whaley Bridge, Audenshaw, Wildboarclough, Congleton and Appleton. It has no apparent zodiacal formation, but roughly at its centre is Alderley Edge, which most people who know about these things reckon to be a place of power. Ask what this circle is about or how it can physically be identified and you get rather hazy answers involving signs on rocks, ancient ritual sites unknown to archaeologists, certain stones and certain trees. The clues are strictly for those with eyes to see.

And what happens within the circle? Well, you are told, there are above the average number of ghostly manifestations, UFO sightings and similar phenomena. 'The trouble is,' Mrs. Rogers says, 'that we accept these things as normal and it becomes very difficult to put this across to ordinary people.'

In some way, a number of sensitive areas, known simply as power points, are linked by and within the circle. These power points are also referred to as 'magnetic centres.' But how do you define magnetism in this context? 'We think,' says Mrs. Rogers, 'that certain spots were charged. Witches believe there are places where several worlds—like the worlds of fairies and spirits—run parallel. These are the spots where they overlap—the chinks in the armour.'

These chinks can, it seems, be identified not only by people who have a spiritual interest in such matters. They can be discovered by, for instance, an experienced dowser using a divining rod or a pendulum or nothing at all—because it is not the implement but something within the dowser himself that reacts to these strange signals.

Science is also catching up with the principle of terrestrial forces. Folk arts like dowsing, which can be seen to produce tangible results, are no longer universally dismissed with academic contempt. But any discussion about alleged subtle influences from the earth must begin with a look back at the time when science, technology and religion were all part of the same thing—the business of survival.

We are learning more—and feel able to speculate considerably more —about the religions of the Bronze Age, some four thousand years ago, when men became obsessed with lugging large stones across the landscape, assembling crude circles and heaping earth into conical mounds. We are beginning to discover how, in physical terms, certain wondrous monuments were raised, but we are still at the speculation stage when it comes to why. And if you want to get a feeling for those arcane ceremonies that so charged an ancient Briton's emotions, you might as well consult a witch — who would claim to be spiritually descended from some pre-Celtic priesthood — as a physicist, historian or archaeologist.

A vast amount has been written over the past twenty years about the alleged complexity of ancient British thinking and the capacity of unshaven hut dwellers to master advanced mathematical and astronomical principles. Were sophisticated engineering techniques used in positioning places of worship according to the arrangement of the stars or the timing of the solstices? And, if so, why were these Neolithic masterminds still basically unshaven hut dwellers? Were they helped by silver-suited super-beings from somewhere slightly to the left of Alpha Centauri . . . ? Perhaps the theories involving both prehistoric computer-programming and extra-terrestrial intervention, attractively-argued though they may be, underestimate the simple power of instinct. Our remote ancestors, dependent upon the whims of Mother Nature for their very survival, were obviously closer to the organism of their environment than we, with our comfortably-dulled perception, can comprehend. If there were forces to be harnessed, channelled or generated, whether for land fertility or as a source of personal energy, they would probably be forces man could sense. Perhaps the dowser's art uses what remains of this ability.

The scientist Lyall Watson, who has been attempting to explain various apparently-supernatural phenomena within the parameters of modern scientific thought, noted how flies appeared to gather in swarms not because of a need to be together but as a collective response to certain landmarks. Church steeples (often towering above ancient sacred sites) seem to have a magnetic attraction for flies. Similarly it has been noticed that farm animals choose certain spots in which to congregate and to sleep, as if they know that a particular area affects their well-being. Watson remarks in *Gifts of Unknown Things* that 'very often cattle gather at that part of a field already selected at some earlier time by man for the erection of a standing stone or a round barrow.'

The suggestion that men and animals feed off much the same spiritual charges is reflected in legends like the one surrounding the siting of Winwick church on Cheshire's northern border. The church allegedly was so positioned because the builders were led there by squealing pigs (making a noise not unlike 'wee-nick, wee-nick'). And it is interesting to note that the church is named after St. Oswald, who has several other local associations — his holy well is nearby — and has strong links with healing. The church site's claim to pagan sanctity is supported by its own elevation and the proximity of Bronze Age burial mounds (see *Mysterious Lancashire*).

Lyall Watson believes that 'we share a common sensitivity with many other species and are able to respond in some way to a set of stimuli that give certain places, and only those places, a necessary, special and magical quality. . . . The choice of such places for settlement or worship is always the result of inspiration rather than intellection.' And therefore our reactions to them today are based on the same indefinable impulse, the origins of which are buried deep in mankind's collective subconscious and conditioned by race-memory. Watson is only echoing what folklore has already told us time and again — and what some people can apparently learn without the benefit of theories at places like Alderley Edge.

People and places, it could be argued, respond to each other. And while certain 'holy shrines' may leave us cold, other places, like the Edge, have retained their magic through continuous human response or ritual repeated over the centuries. The constant spirit of the place overcomes the vagaries of mood and climate. The example most often cited in this context is Glastonbury in Somerset, where Christian and pagan traditions collide and, some would say, come close to reconciliation. The power point of Glastonbury is the Tor, weirdly-conical one-time centre of sun worship; its magnetism is evoked by Dion Fortune in *Avalon of the Heart*.

'There are times,' wrote the famous psychologist-mystic, 'when the power tides of the Unseen flow straight down upon our earth and there are places upon her surface where the channels are open and they come through in the fulness of power. This was known to them of old time . . . and they availed themselves of both time and place when they sought to awaken the higher consciousness.'

The Edge is just like that, according to Edna, a dowser and psychometrist from Manchester. It's as if nature's own life-force is enriched, intensifying the emanations from flowers and stress and, as Garner seemed to indicate, the very mineral strata from which they sprout. 'Going through the woods at Alderley I felt reactions with my hands at various places,' Edna said. 'Vibrations. Like pins and needles. It's a happy, positive feeling.'

IV
GOING STRAIGHT

SHERWOOD FOREST was never big enough for Robin Hood. Reported appearances of the greenclad hero can be traced throughout Cheshire, Derbyshire, Yorkshire, Lancashire and the Lake District: a fairly extensive hunting ground for a man whose chief preoccupation was apparently repossessing feudal revenue from the sheriff of Nottingham. By most accounts Robin was a God-fearing soul, never averse to sharing a side of stolen venison with passing clergy. But this would hardly account for his connection with so many traditionally-sacred spots. Holy wells and old stone crosses bear his name; so do ritual burial places. In Cheshire alone there are at least two ancient sites linked with the altruistic archer—Werneth Low and a tumulus at Tilstone Fearnall known locally as Robin Hood's Tump.

The Werneth legend highlights Robin's previously-unsung prowess as a hurler of large rocks. It is said that a stone missile projected by the outlaw from the top of the Low landed in the Tame near Arden Mill and still bears the impression of the outlaw's sinewy fingers. A round barrow once stood on Werneth Low and it has been named as a sacred site by present-day witches.

Witches have also adopted Robin himself. They regard him as a high priest of his coven of merrie men, with Maid Marian as priestess. And there may well be something here to help uncover the outlaw's true identity. For a likely explanation is that Robin Hood conceals or perpetuates the image of some archetypal figure—perhaps the Green Man of woodland lore, perhaps Cernunnos, the Celtic horned god worshipped by contemporary covens. Certainly Marian fits the mould of an established goddess-image, identified as the pagan Earth Mother and the Christian Virgin: Maid Marian—Virgin Mary; the Medieval Christianisation is implicit. But aside from this speculation there are other, more practical interpretations of the Robin Hood legends, seen particularly clearly in the Tilstone Fearnal story.

The Tilstone Tump tale is more characteristic, if only slightly more credible, than the Werneth Low link, in that it features Robin in his traditional role as master bowman. It is said that he stood atop the Tilstone tumulus in order to aim an arrow at nearby Beeston Crag, which is clearly visible from the mound. If this is true, then stories of Robin's superhuman strength cannot have been exaggerated. For the distance between the two points is around two miles. Shooting an arrow two miles into a solid rock face might also be counted one of Robin's more futile feats. However, those who scoff may envisage the arrow but miss the point. For the significance of the legend probably lies along the flightpath.

In *Traditions and Customs of Cheshire*, Christina Hole remarked that Robin 'could not very well have missed the mark since the crag and barrow are in a dead straight line.' As virtually any two inter-visible spots may be joined by a dead straight line it must be assumed that Miss Hole was indicating the presence of at least one other identifiable point on this alignment. And so here we come to the significance of the legend and, inevitably, to the controversial subject of ley lines.

*   *   *   *

The path of the arrow — or indeed the Werneth stone — offers a clear example of the principle of leys. They are dead straight lines linking sites known and, in most cases venerated, in prehistoric times. All over the world sacred sites appear to have been deliberately aligned, and nowhere is the pattern more apparent than in Britain. Alfred Watkins of Hereford is believed to have been the first modern Briton to uncover the pattern, working way back in the 1920s with a blend of scholarship and perception verging on the visionary. Since then an increasing throng of converts have sought to lay bare the greater pattern under the disapproving nose of the archaeological establishment.

While Derbyshire has dozens of convincing leys, neighbouring Cheshire is typically more guarded with its evidence. Nevertheless the dedicated hunter can find mile after mile of Cheshire's 'old straight track' once he knows where to begin. But before setting out it is useful to look at some of the more recent speculation and discoveries about the nature of prehistoric lines linking stones, mounds, moats and churches across the plain and into the hills.

The official line taken by Watkins was that leys (so called because the suffix 'ley' frequently occurs in place-names along the lines) were trading routes offering the most expedient access to sources of food and minerals and visually marked out for the Neolithic commercial traveller by mounds and stones aligned with hilltops and beacons, the light from which was reflected in various moats and ponds. Into this trading category Watkins placed the earliest Cheshire salt roads, noting that place names ending in Wick or Wich (Nantwich, Northwich, Middlewich) denoted areas of salt production and transit. But salt traditionally is a sacred substance (Cheshire people used to swear on salt instead of the Bible) and the leys, too, appear to have a more hallowed history.

Watkins almost certainly realised this. He appears to have been sensitive to influences unrevealed (except between the lines and in the use of certain imagery) in his books *The Old Straight Track* and its forerunner *Ancient British Trackways*. And the excitement with which Watkin's findings were seized, the zeal with which people who had no previous interest in matters archaeological set out to uncover their own alignments, shows the theory appealed to more than scholarly instincts.

Esoteric doctrines have always talked of ancient power centres. The ley revelations put the idea into a new perspective. Dion Fortune's novels were devoted to explaining arcane secrets, and in *The Goat-Foot*

God, written in the early 1930s, a character is given advice on how to find a suitable property in which to carry out mystical experiments. 'Get a large ordnance map,' he is told, 'and look for standing stones and hammer pools. Standing stones are the sighting marks on these lines of force between the power centres. The stones on the high places and the hammer pools in the bottoms. Water shows up in a valley bottom among trees where stones wouldn't. You sight from one to another and get a dead straight line across country.'

And so the leys mark 'lines of force.' The force is seen as some kind of terrestrial energy. A power which, in its positive phases, improved fertility and aroused psychic activity. An etheric substance, perhaps ebbing and flowing in response to cosmic influences and having magnetic properties.

This power is linked by some researchers with the flow of underground water. Points at which subterranean streams cross are said to be particularly potent energy centres and standing stones have often (some say almost invariably) been sited above such points. Many dowsers now believe it is this force, apparently moving in spirals, which governs their reactions. John Williams, a dowser and ley-researcher from Abergavenny, who has carried out endless experiments with the divining rod and pendulum at ancient sites and believes the force is detectable in menhirs and the stones of so-called burial chambers, has been involved in scientific experiments to measure its magnetic properties. Williams believes the force moves through a stone according to a spiral pattern which changes direction six days after a new moon. This, he says, is when the spiral is at its weakest. But it then builds up until it is powerful enough to cause a 'sensitive' person to bounce off the stone (see Appendix).

The force has also been connected, principally by the writer John Michell, with what the Chinese call feng shui—a harmonising element between the worlds of man and nature which in some parts of the Far East, is consulted even today before a site is chosen for any kind of building, from temples to factories.

But if a mysterious force does flow across the landscape, how was it used? And which existed first—the lines of power or the lines of ancient monuments? A recent suggestion is that the original diversion of energy into straight lines might have been a bad move. After all, nothing in nature is governed by such strict geometry. Authors Janet and Colin Bord think valuable earth-energy may have been drained away by being forced to flow artificially.

It has also been suggested that leys link natural earthly power points in much the same way as, according to oriental belief (now widely supported by Western physicians), acupuncture points are connected by the so-called 'meridiens.' And legends like the Robin Hood tales may indicate this relationship—appreciated thousands of years ago—between two sites of significance.

In many cases such legends are the only remaining evidence of these forgotten terrestrial arteries. The landscape patterns have been fractured, the picture altered, defaced, redrawn and repainted in harsh modern tones. Any present day plan of old alignments is inevitably incomplete. The number of prehistoric constructions still on view in Cheshire may be a small fraction of the number long since obliterated. Nevertheless the 1:50,000 Ordnance Survey map displays enough information for a number of linear patterns to be etched in. Alignments in Cheshire can be plotted with reference to the following features, most of them conveniently marked in Gothic print.

Tumuli

Or round barrows, tumps, toots, etc. Regular mounds, often crowning hill tops, they are the most common of the structures attributed to Bronze Age Britons. Archaeologists describe them (inadequately) as mere burial mounds because they are often found to contain funerary urns or the remains of human bodies. But, as Christina Hole pointed out in *Traditions and Customs of Cheshire,* they are sometimes quite empty and seem to have functioned more as landmarks.

Sadly, most of Cheshire's tumuli have been squashed into comparative insignificance. Many—including Robin Hood's Tump—are not featured on the OS map. However, a number of the neglected sites can be marked in with the aid of one of the Cheshire Archaeological Bulletins, published locally, which contain lists of investigated sites complete with map references.

Robin Hood's Tump has another feature prominent in ley lore—a lone Scots pine. Watkins noticed that these distinctively tall trees often occurred, either in isolation or in small clumps, on alignments, a fact picked up by Christina Hole who wrote: 'In early times single trees had a sacred character. Solitary Scotch firs in conspicuous positions served as . . . landmarks along the prehistoric straight tracks and clumps of them are often found on barrows—as at Tilstone Fearnall.'

If Robin Hood's Tump is marked on the map and a line run from it through Beeston Castle crag it picks up at least two other sites within a few miles. Tumuli around Alderley Edge also fall into lines. Traditions also indicate a ritual significance of mounds, especially those on hill tops. Toot Hill, near Macclesfield, which was crowned by a tumulus, was associated with a local fire festival.

Castle Sites

The spots chosen for castles often indicate a need for spiritual as well as physical security. Sites marked on the OS map as 'mottes' are usually castle mounds, often enlarged tumuli marking sacred as well as important strategic points . . . as emphasised by their frequent proximity to churches. An interesting example is the Malpas mound, immediately behind the church in the centre of the South Cheshire hill town. It forms the axis of several notable alignments. It should be noted that quite a lot of mounds labelled 'motte' bear no trace of castle building.

Moats

Moats are the most common ancient remains on the Cheshire plain. Watkins saw them as part of what he called a 'fairy chain,' reflecting sunlight or beacon fires along the leys. Nowadays we tend to think of moats as purely defensive ditches, but in fact most of them are

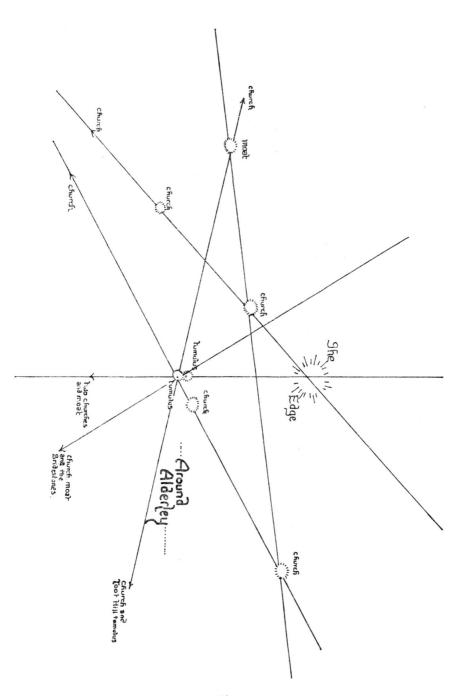

church

church

church

church

moat

church

church

tumulus

The

Edge

two churches
and moat

tumulus

church

church moat
and the
Bridestones.

Around
Alderley

church and
Toot Hill tumulus

21

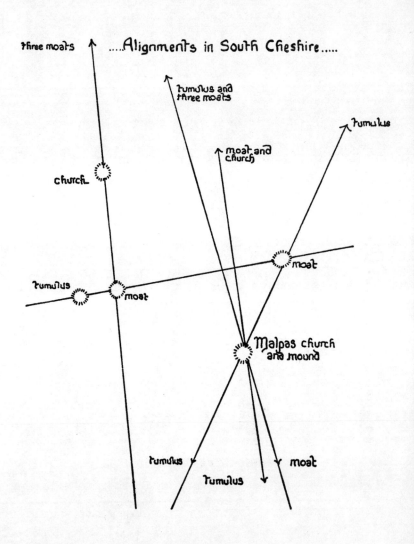

....Alignments in South Cheshire.....

three moats

tumulus and
three moats

tumulus

moat and
church

church

moat

tumulus

moat

Malpas church
and mound

tumulus

moat

Tumulus

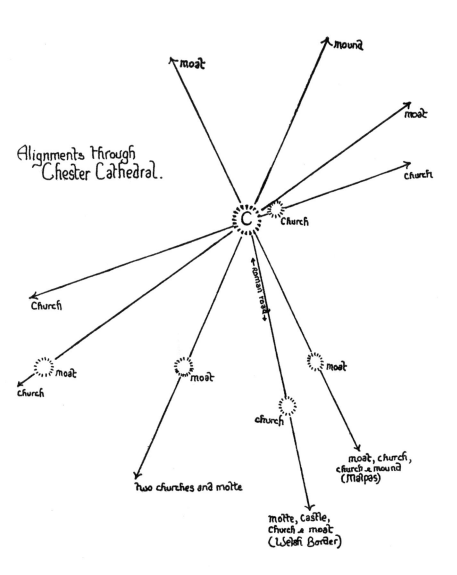

Alignments Through
Chester Cathedral.

moat

mound

moat

church

Church

Church

Roman road

moat

moat

moat

church

church

two churches and motte

moat, church,
church & mound
(Malpas)

motte, castle,
church & moat
(Welsh Border)

very ancient, often formed when earth was thrown up into circular mounds, and greatly predating the buildings many of them now enclose. Almost every moat on the Cheshire map falls into some kind of alignment—frequently three in a row aligned with some elevated site. Four moats can be traced on a ley leading from the western outskirts of Tarporley to Knowl Hill, near Buckley in Clwyd. Another four occur on an offshoot of this alignment leading south-east and three moats align within two miles on a ley from Knowl Hill to the church-side mound at Aldford.

Churches

Cheshire has a vast number of churches with origins lost in the mists of antiquity. It is believed that most early Christian churches were built on or near focal points of pagan worship. For the newly-baptised Britons would no doubt have been unwilling to let slip their land-related religion for one which offered no practical alternative to the tested methods of ensuring field fertility. It seems likely that the philosophy of the new faith was grafted onto the techniques of the old— hence the fusion of pagan and Christian festivals. Ideals were, and still are, quite compatible as far as country dwellers are concerned.

We can see that a number of Cheshire churches are situated on or next to ancient mounds. We also know that a large number of comparatively modern church buildings replaced earlier ones with pre-Norman origins . . . themselves erected on pagan sites. Chester Cathedral is said to occupy the site of a sun temple. And we can now see that dozens of churches are aligned with each other and with mounds and moats. We also have several legends indicating that the most important thing about churches is the land they occupy. Inspiration, visions and supernatural interference appear to have been key factors in the selection of temple points. The essence of this is preserved in folk tales.

The legendary origins of Winwick church have already been discussed. A comparable story emanates from Over, whose church was originally in the centre of the village and is now a mile away. As soon as the builders had finished work, but prior to consecration, it was apparently carried off by the Devil. But the monks of Vale Royal discovered the theft and sounded their bells, which so startled Satan that he dropped the edifice where it now stands. Stoak church was also shifted by the Devil and Ince church was carried off by fairies during its construction. The details fall into regular folklorish patterns, repeated throughout Britain (see *Mysterious Lancashire*). What is significant is the belief in supernatural aid to the selection of a site, which may hide more fundamental techniques allied to dowsing.

Hill Forts

Almost every early religion held hill tops to be sacred—places of communion with higher powers. But there is no denying their strategic importance in tribal warfare, and so hill-top earthworks tend to be classed as forts. On this level they seem to be the most obvious and uncomplicated of prehistoric structures. Archaeologists have shown that they were used in battle over thousands of years, extending into

24

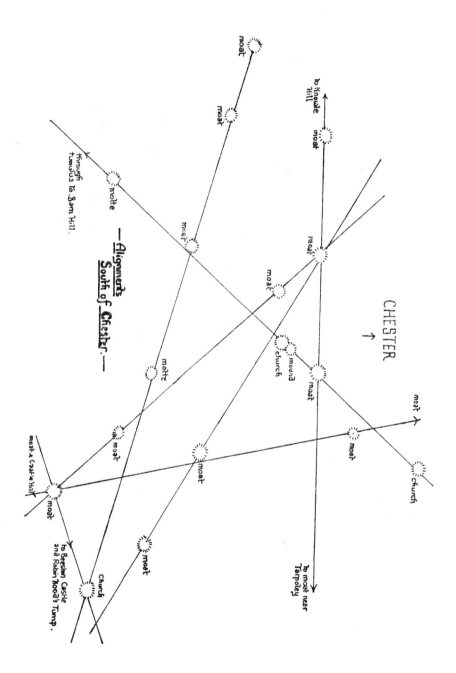

— *Alignments South of Chester* —

CHESTER →

moat

moat

to Kinsale Hill
moat

through tumulus to Bam Hill.
motte

moat

moat

moat

moat

mound
church

moat

motte

moat

moat

moat

moat

moat near Castle Hill
through
moat

to Beeston Castle and Robin Hood's Tump.

church

church

moat ↑

moat

to moat near Tarporley

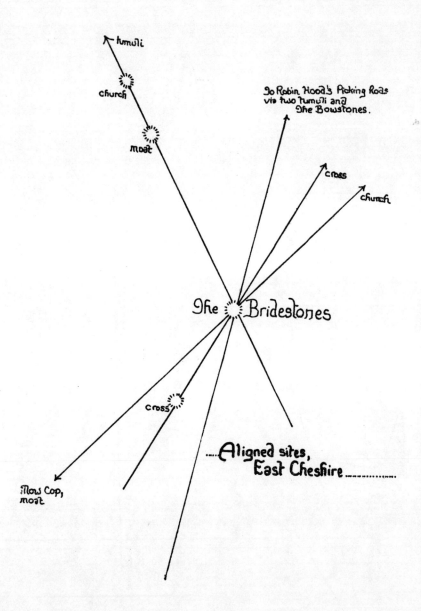

tumuli

church

moat

To Robin Hood's Picking Rods
via two tumuli and
The Bowstones.

cross

church

The :: Bridestones

cross

Mow Cop,
moat

.....Aligned sites,
East Cheshire.............

Saxon and Norman times. But do their origins lie entirely within the confines of military history? In a detailed examination of camps and forts in his *Cheshire Before the Romans*, W. J. Varley says the general distribution of hill forts was apparently restricted—a fact which puzzled him. Some areas 'where every hill top cries out for a hill fort' are mysteriously bare. It has also been pointed out that many of these fortified areas are too large to have been adequately defended and the term 'fort' is sometimes softened to 'camp.'

The Cheshire plain can be surveyed extensively from hill forts in the county's central highlands. There is evidence that these sites played their parts in the ley pattern and the beacon system which unified the county. Lines of moats and churches spray out from Kelsborrow Castle and Maiden Castle (on Bickerton Hill). The Helsby and Foxhill forts occur on minor alignments. But Eddisbury camp, on the edge of Delamere Forest, has no obvious connections with other sites.

Crosses

It is widely assumed that crosses are the natural successors of prehistoric standing stones. Certainly Celtic crosses, particularly in Cornwall, have clearly been fashioned from existing menhirs. But it is unsafe to assume all crosses, regardless of antiquity, have megalithic ancestors. However, some—especially in rural areas—quite clearly mark the crossings of alignments or the paths to major centres of worship, and references to headless crosses may sometimes indicate standing stones. In Cheshire, note The Bowstones, monolithic remains of ancient 'boundary markers' on a long ley terminating at two similar monuments, Robin Hood's Picking Rods in North Derbyshire.

But the most impressive crosses in the county—and, in fact, in Britain—are those in the centre of Sandbach. They appear to have been erected as far back as the eighth century—supposedly 'raised on the spot where a priest from Northumberland first preached Christianity,' said Alfred Rimmer in *Ancient Stone Crosses of England* (1875). The extensive, intricately-hewn designs on the crosses suggest both Christian and pagan influences and Rimmer pointed out similarities with monuments on the Isle of Iona and in Ireland . . . also indicating an ancient Celtic link via the Wirral:

'The Sandbach crosses (wrote Rimmer) seem at first to be curious isolated memorials and they are all the more interesting from there being so very little that resembles them in that part of England; on this account some very curious Runic crosses which have been discovered at West Kirby are worthy of note. The class of sculpture, though common in Scotland and Ireland and not unknown in the Isle of Man, is rare in England. It would seem not to be without connecting links, however, for opposite to the West Kirby cross was Hilbre Island, at the mouth of the Dee, easily approached at low water over the celebrated Dee sands. . . .'

And here, noted Alfred Rimmer, was found another cross, which, according to local expert Mr. Eckroyd Smith, was 'similar in design to several found in Ireland and the Isle of Man.' The island itself once housed a cell of Cistercian monks connected with Chester Cathedral. And 'there is hardly a doubt,' says Rimmer, that West Kirby was once the site of 'some old temple of which all record has long since perished.'

The Sandbach crosses, however, are of limited use to the ley-hunter. They have been re-erected on the present site and probably did not originally stand in close proximity to each other.

Roman Roads

Watkins was loth to undermine the Romans' reputation as master surveyors and road-builders. But he chanced his arm and suggested that many Roman roads simply followed, when possible, the existing remains of old straight tracks. He imagined the invaders arriving in a Britain where the ley system was still perceptible, where lines in more accessible areas had been trampled into roads still used by the Britons. Why should they not take advantage of these existing routes, reinforcing them in their own way for military purposes? In the same way, of course, the Romans would not hesitate to deviate from the old routes where expedient, and so Roman roads are perhaps better kept as confirmation of already-established leys.

Two examples spring to the eye on the Chester 1:50,000 OS map. You can pick up a Roman road just south of Chester city centre which joins a clear ley from the cathedral, through Eccleston church, Aldford motte, Castletown castle site and Shocklach church to a moat at Tallarn Green, just over the Welsh border. Another Roman road, leading out of Malpas, follows for more than half a mile the ley from Malpas church and mound, through a tumulus at Coddington and two moats to Chester Cathedral (two other moats at either end of the line make this a fairly impressive example).

The intrepid historian and Arthurian researcher S. G. Wildman throws out some hints for the ley-hunter in his book *The Black Horsemen* when he refers to several curiously-parallel 'green roads' on the Wirral. Wildman and colleagues tracked these lines (discovering evidence of more than a score of ancient bridges across streams and brooks) across miles of countryside, convinced they fitted somehow into the pattern of Roman roads in the area. One expert concluded they could have been 'practice roads' used by the Romans for training purposes, but they may have earlier and more intriguing origins.

Place-Names

An unreliable but interesting method of identifying possible ley-points where all physical evidence has vanished. For instance:

> Ley lines around Alderley Edge feature churches, moats and tumuli. Every gothic-labelled site in this area is linked with at least two other points. Except for one — a tumulus in the grounds of Capesthorne Hall, about three miles south of the Edge. This apparent outsider can be brought into play by pinpointing the unmarked tumulus site on Yearns Low, near Rainow, about five miles north-east of Capesthorne. It can be brought further into the pattern if a line is drawn upwards through the lower of the

28

two tumuli, a mile north of Capesthorne near Birtles Hall. If this line is extended to the grounds of Mottram Old Hall, another two and a half miles, it can be seen to cross three places with names suggesting ancient markers — Mottram Cross, Shaw Cross and The Mount, Hare Hill.

V

ELF PATHS

ELF roads through Cheshire provide a convenient escape route for the heroes of Alan Garner's children's book *The Wierdstone of Brisingamen.* It seems the nature of these thoroughfares renders travellers invisible to ordinary mortals. Or at least to mortals who do not accidentally stray across the path. . . .

This is an old idea, not confined to fictional fairy stories. If there are real elf roads, then they are ley lines. And elves themselves are as real as anyone wants to make them. The latest literature on the subject suggests we create elves and fairies for ourselves. People who see them (and everyone has heard of somebody who claims to have) are picking up reflections of thought-forms from their own subconscious minds.

If you accept this you then come to the question: how real is a thought-form? The late Tom Lethbridge, archaeologist and dowser, and one of his greatest fans, the writer Colin Wilson, suggest that the remains of one person's thought-forms can be seen by another, particularly in certain places — on power points, within psychic force-fields and, of course, on leys (although Lethbridge himself had clearly not come across the ley theories). Images, emotions, sensations can be imprinted on the 'psychic ether' and picked up at places where, as Mrs. Rogers puts it, 'worlds overlap.'

We have seen, for instance, how Roman roads sometimes follow the routes of leys. And it is interesting to relate this to the innumerable stories about people who, finding themselves on a stretch of road initially laid by the Romans, have seemed to hear the tramp of legionaries' boots and see a procession of weary warriors, uttering morose curses about the English weather and seemingly oblivious of the Ford Cortina in the lay-by. Fairies and elves, however, seem to be connected not with the emotional imprints of people long dead, but with the life-energies in the vegetation which, as most people would agree, pulses harder in some places than in others. If you spot a fairy in the desert, you are both in trouble!

But, it seems, when you walk along what we now call a ley, you might become exposed to phenomena not normally associated with your usual plane of existence. Something tips the balance of your normal perception. And the senses, thus jogged, clothe these pulses of unusual energy with convenient images from the subconscious. The images are archetypal; a 'sensitive' person on a ley line might 'see' a nature spirit as surely as a drunk sees pink elephants . . . except that one comes from a heightened rather than obscured awareness.

We saw earlier how animals seem to take for granted certain energy patterns. Dion Fortune, writing about Glastonbury Tor, says: 'Something which no eye can see drives the cattle down from the hill and they do not fly from it in panic but go quietly and orderly.' It has often been noticed how cattle not only congregate at certain points, as Lyall Watson observed, but also enter and leave fields by particular routes. Often farm gates are placed according to these bovine whims and it is one explanation of why so many standing stones have been converted in centuries past into gateposts. And gates and stiles have a mythology of their own — especially in Cheshire.

'It would seem that stiles and gates were a favourite haunt for Cheshire boggarts,' writes Jacqueline Simpson in her *Folklore of the Welsh Border*. Now a boggart is a northcountry entity who appears in dozens of disguises. He absorbs most of the accepted characteristics of fairies and of ghosts, sometimes with poltergeist-like tendencies to vandalism. Mostly he's an elemental spirit, attached to various features of the countryside. And in Cheshire boggarts appear to guard the secret paths.

Jacqueline Simpson recalls the story of a boy and a farm labourer who are about to cross a stile in Cheshire. They have to stand aside to allow a little man, around four feet in height, to cross from the other side. As the diminutive figure reaches the top of the stile it begins to expand alarmingly until the two witnesses quit the scene in terror. 'My informant was perfectly confident that it was a boggart they had seen and remained so all his life,' said the man who collected the tale at first hand.

There are many others like it. The Reverend Francis Kilvert, himself possessed of an almost paranormal perception of nature's deeper aspects, recorded in his famous diary the story of a similar entity which haunted a stile. And Alfred Watkins, working in the same border area, found dozens of examples of old field gates and stiles, unchanged since time immemorial, which marked the passage of obvious leys. It was Watkins who also discovered another guardian of the leys — the hermit who ties in so closely with the image of the wizard of Alderley, with his monkish robes and staff. Hermits' caves or cells were often found to be adjacent to long-distance leys and Watkins even suggested that the man with the stave is an image of the original Bronze Age surveyors who marked out the lines, sighting along the straight pole in the same way that Watkins himself often did.

More recently, Paul Screeton, a sub-editor on a daily paper in the North East and former editor of the Ley Hunter magazine, told of an unexpected meeting on a ley line with a strange brownish entity about three feet high which appeared momentarily and then hopped out of his life forever. Such manifestations, said Screeton in his book *Quicksilver Heritage*, were connected with the obviously psychic aspects of the earth force.

But meetings on leys are not always friendly encounters. Anglican exorcist Dom Robert Petit-Pierre warns that it may be dangerous to assume that all influences and emanations from the countryside are essentially beneficial. Ley lines, he says, are neutral; mere pipelines for vibrations. Bad energy stored in leys can be mentally and physically debilitating, like the energy from the Alderley 'black spot' referred to earlier. Such points in the landscape seem to invite suicide or violence, which, of course, reinforces their power. Jacqueline Simpson tells of Black Hill in Cheshire where a murder was committed and grass refuses to grow. What came first — the murder or the peculiar deadness of the place?

The dowser T. C. Lethbridge referred to negative atmospheric conditions as 'ghouls,' force-fields of evil or depression, and talked of a particular cliff in Devon, from which people were always being tempted to jump. Janet Bord, an author who has made an extensive study of ancient sites and ley centres all over Britain, said: 'At certain sites I've had the misfortune to be gripped by terrible pains in my insides. As it only happens at ancient sites I can only think it must be something to do with the energies there.'

Dom Robert Petit-Pierre thinks the church should renew its links with earth-energies — links which are in fact still echoed in ceremonies like beating the bounds, in which parish boundaries, often marked out by ancient stones and crosses, are traditionally blessed. This is clearly a hangover from the days when the early bishops deliberately installed their churches on or close to pagan centres of worship. Says Dom Robert: 'I believe in going round and giving the ley lines a blessing — a clean-up.' This ley-laundering, he says, should be done at the great seasonal festivals, beginning in February with Candlemass.

As an exorcist, Dom Robert would no doubt find significant elements in a story dating back to February 1564, which might be an illustration of the kind of thing that can happen to people on ley lines. It occurred at Chester and was retold by Edward Baines in his massive work on the history of Lancashire. Anne Milner, 'a maiden of Chester, eighteen years of age,' was innocently bringing in her father's cattle from the field when 'an evil spirit appeared to her in the form of a white thing encompassing her round about.' Anne just wasn't the same after this. The following morning she took to her bed where 'she fell into a succession of trances.' It wasn't until a month later, after a clergyman, Master Lane, had made her say the Lord's Prayer and the Te Deum, that she made a recovery. This case caused something of a stir at the time and Sir William Calverley and other notables 'attested to its veracity.'

There is a tradition that sacred sites, and therefore, presumably, the paths of power linking one to another, are equipped with 'guardians.' It's a concept taken for granted by witches and occultists as an explanation of the apparently malevolent entities said to attach themselves to people who stray into realms where they don't belong. Elementals feed on the power-of-place like the traditional familiar at the witch's breast. They can be attached to cult-objects found at archaeological digs — as in the case of a hairy horror straight from the old Boris Karloff movies which seemed to be connected to two Celtic heads brought into the home of Britain's most eminent Celtic scholar Dr. Anne Ross. They were moved out, on the advice of a clergyman.

But what exactly are the so-called guardians guarding? In most

A modern inn-sign on Alderley Edge recalls an ancient legend.

King witch Alex Sanders at work on Alderley Edge — a still from
the documentary film 'Legend of the Witches.'

Ancient symbolism — the crosses of Sandbach.

Robin Hood's Tump — with its lonesome pine.

The Edge — steeped in occult lore.

The view from the Bridestones.

Winwick church — site of pagan sanctity.

The face of The Wizard hewn from the rockface at Alderley Edge.

The modern replacement cross at Marton — one of Cheshire's medieval churches.

stories it's 'hidden treasure' — of the kind that the wizard of Alderley, one of the more amiable guardians, gave to the farmer from Mobberley in return for his horse. Less-savoury characters guard the hidden hoard of Richard II, said to lie at the bottom of a deep well in Beeston Castle rock. Many people over the centuries tried to reach it, according to Christina Hole's *Traditions and Customs of Cheshire,* but were put to flight by the guardians — 'terrible demons' which appeared whenever anybody got beyond a certain depth. 'So frightful was their appearance that cases were cited of men who had died from sheer horror immediately after seeing them,' wrote Miss Hole.

More sophisticated searchers, armed with modern technology, made a final attempt quite recently to find the king's gold. They didn't encounter any demons, but then, they didn't get the loot either. It was concluded that no treasure was there. But wells, strange shafts and things at the bottom of them, are a significant part of Celtic magical lore. Possibly this legend has roots beyond the days of Richard II. And it leads us to another 'guardian' story which opens better channels of inquiry.

VI

THE MEDDLER AND THE STONES

MAYBE it was something to do with the day—freezing February with an east wind whipping up a trailer for the evening blizzard. On such a day the stones gleam greyly out of dank foliage and it is hard to avoid sliding back through the years into the shaking shoes of the farmer who dared take a spade to Cheshire's most imposing ancient monument.

The Bridestones hold up two giant fingers from the hills beyond Congleton; a frosty V-sign to those who might fracture their petrified peace. Somehow, even in kinder weather, they are slightly ominous. The locals, according to the Congleton Chronicle in 1947, regarded them still with 'awe and reverence.' But perhaps the main reason for the reverence dates back to the early years of the nineteenth century and a link with ancient pagan magic.

A Neolithic chambered tomb. That's how today's archaeologists describe the Bridestones. The chamber, they say, was once covered with earth. A fairly well preserved but otherwise unremarkable site. But nearly two hundred years ago the stones were a source of greater mystery. It was believed that a treasure lay hidden beneath them. Such was the local regard for pagan sanctity, however, that no-one had been inclined to dig for it ... for it was said that a king and queen were also buried here and anyone who disturbed them would die.

But this particular farmer was made of harder stuff. He was unimpressed by superstition. And he happened to own the land, so he moved in with his spade. The details of what happened next were revealed by the farmer's successor and subsequently published in a letter to the Staffordshire Advertiser from an East Cheshire landowner, Mr. J. F. Williams. According to the report the farmer 'began to dig within the enclosure and had not been long employed when he saw something which so frightened him as to disable him and prevent him moving from the spot. All the following night a female figure attired in white apparel visited his house and remained there until morning, turning everything over and over, which circumstance had such effect upon the whole family that they left the farm.'

Asked if the phenomenon had ever recurred, the new owner of the land told Mr. J. F. Williams: 'I never meddle with the stones, sir. . . .'

*   *   *   *

The meddler is not unique. The horny-handed materialist is the sworn enemy of the 'old stones,' wherever they rear their mossy heads. He has appeared throughout recorded history whenever the ancient patterns have clashed with the interests of modern agriculture. Farmers in general have never figured highly as conservationists when commercial considerations have been at stake ... especially in the less-fertile uplands. In rural Wales, where it is estimated that only one third of existing ancient sites have been discovered, hill farmers are still considered a major menace to unprotected archaeological remains. Earthworks are ruthlessly ploughed, hill forts plundered and stones shattered, if not always with fore-knowledge of their significance.

Yet some of these old sites do not appear to have been entirely unprotected, and megalith molesters have received warnings more severe than a nasty letter from the local archaeological trust. Sober British antiquarian records are full of tales recalling unhappy events which befell sundry vandals and robbers of ancient graves. There are stories of savage storms breaking from clear skies at the touch of a shovel, of deaths in the family, expiry of livestock, and of ground, reclaimed from the prehistoric dead, which proved resistant to all known fertilisers and never yielded crops again. Janet and Colin Bord's *The Secret Country* lists some of the phenomena inflicted on meddlers over the centuries and ponders on whether the victims suffered effects similar to those caused by breaking electrical circuitry — a thrust of ancient energy from a node of terrestrial power.

It is said that the leys linking ancient sites are only channels, capable of distributing positive energy but also prone to pollution. They are like telephone wires, according to the Anglican monk and exorcist Dom Robert Petit-Pierre. And the nature of the message depends on who is calling.

Great emotional intensity was generated at rituals practised on power centres. Dom Robert, in a BBC interview, compared it to the kind of excitement built up by a football crowd. 'But they knew how to bottle it up,' he explained. 'Then they let it loose as mental energy at their enemies. It's certain that the leys were used for mental projection.'

It is said that ghosts are images imposed upon the atmosphere by events of massive emotional turbulence. If this can be done accidentally it can also be done deliberately. Ancient deities, for instance, represented elemental forces which, it was believed, could be unleashed by ritual.

The stories and atmosphere surrounding the Bridestones suggest they were subjected, over a long period, to heavy charges of emotional energy. And, it may then be suggested, the farmer fractured some kind of circuit as easily as a roadmender slices through an electric cable. What, then, were the influences at work at the Bridestones? Can anything be uncovered by applying what is known of early religious feeling and ritual practice?

There are two main channels of approach to the secrets of the stones. We can attempt to penetrate the folk-tales surrounding the monument and others like it. And we can trace the associations of the name itself. 'Bridestones' hints immediately at marital relations — also reflected in the local belief that a king and queen are buried here. It also suggests a link — more solidly supported by historical background

Brigantia, the North Country goddess. From an unflattering statue found at Birrens in Southern Scotland.

—with St. Bride, a Christianisation of Brigid, the Celtic mother goddess. Both connections may be equally relevant.

*   *   *   *

The Mother Goddess, in essence still venerated today by millions of Roman Catholics, is probably the oldest British deity—worshipped, it is believed, in the Bronze Age and identified, with a few variations, by the Celts. She appears as the goddess Brigid, mainly in Ireland, and Brigantia in the North of England. Both, says Anne Ross in *Pagan Celtic Britain,* were connected with agriculture, the rearing of animals and yield of the earth. The Earth Mother was a peacetime deity, supervisor of a settled community.

The Brigantes—people involved in the cult of Brigantia—occupied a massive area of the North. Guy Ragland Phillips, in his speculative study of the tribe and its traditions, suggests the Brigantes were descended from some of the very earliest Celtic races—including the Iberians, whose strain he identifies in the 'very dark, short-statured people found in the area of Biddulph Moor, near the Bridestones (see Appendix). It might be assumed therefore that the Bridestones were dedicated to land fertility and the generative process—as perhaps indicated by the two great upright stones, far more phallic than most menhirs.

The name Bridestones is far from unique in the North. Another well-known example on the North York Moors is also a burial chamber. Ragland Phillips notes a second group of Bridestones nearby and a Bride Cross in the same area. Bride sites, he records, often share 'a curious and sinister legend.' The Bride Cross and both groups of stones are said to mark the place where a bride was slain for reasons of infidelity. 'The legend, like some others to be found in the same area, has a ring of human sacrifice long ago,' says Ragland Phillips. In each case, he points out, the woman is said to haunt the area.

Was our farmer followed home by the ghost of a murdered bride in her 'white apparel'? Or by an image representing a string of sacrificial maidens . . . ? It may, in fact, be possible to draw these slim strands of speculation together . . . by recalling the legend of the king and queen supposedly lying beneath the Bridestones. But first some theories about the nature and purpose of burial chambers.

* * * *

Dr. Wilhelm Reich, a farmer's son turned psychoanalyst, died in prison in 1957 after having his books and equipment seized by the vicious watchdogs of the American Food and Drug Administration. The cause of his downfall was his discovery of what he called orgone energy—the great lifeforce, previously explained only by poets and mystics. To a contemptuous public Reich claimed it could not only be seen, photographed and measured but even locked up in boxes. He saw himself 'stepping beyond the intellectual framework of present day character structure and, with that, the civilisation of the last 5,000 years.' His 'primal orgone ocean,' which, he claimed, governed the growth and metabolism of every living thing, washed through land, sea and air and even moved planets. It ebbed and flowed in a ceaseless tide of life. And, when man reached out and related to it, he discovered God. . . .

With the help of colleagues Reich manufactured telephone kiosk-like boxes, which he called 'orgone energy accumulators,' for storing concentrated charges of the life force. They were constructed from alternate layers of organic and inorganic materials and, inside, the effect was one of heightened perception, strange tingling sensations and the blue aura of orgone energy. The development, linked with Reich's remarkable theories on human sexuality, has a significance which has since over-reached the wall of criticism which surrounded his work during his lifetime. It may also help explain the signficance of underground chambers as used by religious groups all over the world for thousands of years.

Hidden chambers have been found under earthmounds, deep in pyramids or beneath the earth itself, where they were used for spiritual and initiation purposes. Entrance tunnels and ante-chambers were often designed to evoke a range of emotions before the inner sanctum was reached. In America the Hopi Indians, whose ancient beliefs are tied in with universal nature concepts, still descend by ladder into dark underground rooms for secret rituals. Construction methods used in ancient Egypt created insulation against unwanted vibrations during initiation ceremonies. Ancient 'burial' chambers throughout the world differ widely in appearance. But they have often manifested an intriguing common feature — being carefully built from materials placed in alternate organic and inorganic layers. The Bridestones chamber, in its original covered form, may therefore have functioned as something rather similar to Dr. Reich's orgone accumulator.

*   *   *   *

The king and queen were important figures in the old cycle of seasonal rituals. They still appear symbolically in the famous May ceremony at Castleton, Derbyshire. In some areas the couple — or at least the king — met a bloody sacrificial end at harvest time at the climax of one of our more gruesome fertility rites. The beginning of the great cycle was Candlemas, which coincided with the feast of Bride, or Brigid. In Scotland, according to C. A. Burland's *Echoes of Magic,* two children assumed the role of king and queen in a ceremony which persisted until quite recently. The pair were carried around the streets in a litter covered with green leaves and ribbons, and the ritual ended with a fire festival. 'One can imagine no more directly Celtic festival for the youth of the year,' says Burland.

Candlemas, then, was the first of the great annual festivals and saw the cranking up of the ancient mechanism that turned the year. It was the time when young people were expected to choose their mates. Relationships would then be ready for consummation on May Day. In *The Avebury Cycle* Michael Dames sees the prehistoric landscape sculpted in accordance with the seasonal fertility rites, with different features reflecting aspects of the cycle . . . culminating in a ceremonial sex act at some major sacred site.

Sexual congress, taking place in contact with the earth, has always been seen as the most obvious method of stimulating fertility in the land. It works with a combination of psycho-sexual energy and sympathetic magic. Could the chamber at the Bridestones, this ancient core of magical power, have been used for such a rite, in which it was believed the generative force would be amplified and channelled into the earth? Were the newly-dubbed king and queen 'buried' here for a ritual consummation in which the psychic energy created at the moment of orgasm became fused with the channels of earth-energy which merged at this spot . . . sending a radiating power into the fields?

Colin Wilson, in *Mysteries,* points out that the king and queen symbols also occur in the arcane science of alchemy. Old alchemical works show pictures of a king and queen lying down together in some kind of bath. In this context they represent the eternal male and female forces which interact to produce a 'higher substance' — possibly the Philosopher's Stone, the mysterious mineral said to act as a catalyst, raising the vibrations of humble matter to the level of higher matter. This is usually seen simply as a question of creating gold from base metals. Or, more profoundly, raising human consciousness to a cosmic level. It could also be applied to land fertility — creating golden corn from base soil.

The use of sexual activity as a means of reaching untapped reservoirs of energy, both physical and spiritual, was the basis of the Eastern Tantric system of self-development in which sexual energy — the Kundalini or serpent power — is made to rise up the spine activating the 'chakras' or bodily energy-centres. The final one is at the top of the head and when the force reaches this point it induces ecstacy and enlightenment. Eastern philosophy sees the human body as a network of energy channels radiating from major and minor power centres. Acupuncture involves the stimulation of certain, often minor, energy points which, when activated, stimulate the body's own healing powers. The parallel with the ley-system is too obvious to miss, and dowser Tom Graves has drawn in the details in his book *Needles of Stone,* in which he suggests standing stones are like the needles of the acupuncturist working at a terrestrial level.

Colin Wilson suggests that the forces used in alchemy, the most complex and closely guarded subject in esoteric history, are the forces of the Earth, which are themselves conditioned by the forces of the heavens — planetary formations and the natural cycles. Hence the use of ancient stones and circles as both power points and planetary observatories. The French alchemist Armand Barbault wrote: 'Not only are there times when nature's life forces are at their most intense, there are also privileged areas where these forces are concentrated.' The alchemist, selecting materials for his work, pays close attention to the country calendar. The planets affect the Earth and the Earth affects man. Thus, to the adept, vast forces are available.

All this is pure speculation. We have no way of knowing to what extent, if any, ancient ceremonies were related to this type of thinking. We don't know how they operated originally or to what extent they were altered, confused or currupted. It is possible that the Bridestones were the focal point of different types of ritual over the centuries, some conceived instinctively for a practical purpose according to a tested formula, others developing later out of superstition and misunderstanding. The one unifying factor seems to have been a persistent belief in the site as a living, potent energy centre which demanded human respect.

*   *   *   *

Postscript

St. Bride, Christian successor of the pagan Brigid, also concerned herself with human fertility. Barren wives would pray to her and, on St. Bride's Day, would attempt to persuade her to enter their homes. Rushes were laid down for the comfort of the frugal saint before the household retired to bed. And it is recorded that, like the apparition which visited the man who meddled with the stones, the white-clad St. Bride was accustomed to stay for the whole of the night. . . .

VII

PRIMITIVE CHESHIRE

THE past few years have seen the spread in Britain of a new paganism, reflected in the soaring interest in ley theories, legends and forgotten forces . . . a search for meaning in a threatened environment. Paganism is the right word. But it's also slightly misleading. The search is for spiritual harmony at a more primitive level. It relates to intuition rather than adherence to doctrine. It is probably not so much a new paganism as the admission of an old paganism that never really went away. The exorcist Dom Robert Petit-Pierre said in a radio interview that he felt it was, on the whole, a positive sign.

It may seem to modern-day ley hunters that they are forging a direct link with the intuitive earth-awareness of the Bronze Age Britons. In fact there is evidence everywhere of a continued awareness, which, during the centuries of repression affecting anything that smelled of magic, was carefully concealed. If we are openly discussing it again it's because the worst that can happen to us is to be labelled cranks. And there's nothing unhealthy about that. After all, some of us *are* cranks.

Nowadays there is an illusory orderliness to life. Its greater schemes are sketched in Whitehall or Brussels; its smaller ones sliding from the well-oiled wheels that remind us to pay our road tax or our rates. Motorways gently lead us in the right direction without recourse to our more primitive senses and heads turn to the capital for news that affects the nation. The basic blueprint of this system can be traced to patterns laid down under the Roman Empire. The fabric of administration, even our present road system, closely follows the grand design of the rational Roman mind. But life in Britain wasn't always like that, and the mysterious faint scent of 'something more' still has us pulling at the leash of civilisation. The dilemma we find ourselves in has been felt many times by our ancestors. The polarities are pinpointed in many ways by the problems of integrating Roman and Celtic civilisations . . . problems which had to be faced in Cheshire.

It was once fashionable to paint a picture of barbarous Britons foolishly fighting the forces of progress in the shape of the advancing Roman invasion. Evidence suggests, however, that the Celts maintained a civilisation in many ways more mature, humane and democratic than any of the achievements of their conquerors. Professor Jean Markale, hailed as the greatest living authority on Celtic history, compared the two with the opposing forces in the pioneer struggles on the American frontier—when farmers, obsessed with order and barbed wire, tried to crush the cattlemen who wanted to be free to roam the range. If environment shapes national characteristics, argued Markale, then the

Celts, in their pastel landscapes of moorlands, meadows and mists, looked at life from the cosmic point of view, while the Romans, used to sharp Mediterranean sunlight, saw only a rational two-tone world of light and shadow. Our innermost feelings inevitably relate to the Celtic culture in which intuitive reactions form a way of life geared to nature and the cycle of the seasons.

It used to be assumed that the Celtic priests, the Druids, were responsible for the raising of standing stones and the construction of ancient mounds. We now know, from modern dating techniques, that these monuments belonged to an earlier culture. But it is not entirely inaccurate to refer to ancient sites, as the Victorians did, as 'Druidical temples.' If the Druids did not actually erect the monuments, they at least inherited them. And they also inherited the system of knowledge, built upon instinctive earth-consciousness, which led to their construction. The Druids used the sites and they used the system; they were probably its last 'official' custodians. And, thanks to them, the old ways thrived in the wilderness of the North West of England long after the coming of Christianity. The reliance on magic was never really abandoned. The area had its own links with The Source. And it may still hold on to them.

Scholars deny that there was a 'System' of knowledge, because to them there can have been no knowledge without the written word. But to the Druids the kind of knowledge you could write down wouldn't have been worth preserving. What was preserved, and still to some extent remains, was a mechanism for living. A wheel of life was turned by ritual, powered by a fusion of energies. It had four gears to increase the motion, the rate of vibration. They were the four points on the Celtic calendar: Samhain, Imbolc, Beltaine and Lugnasadh. Cheshire has retained many traditions and threads of folklore which, if often tangled, are still firmly tied to these feast days.

*   *   *   *

The new year began on November 1st, Samhain, whose eerie echoes now reverberate as Hollowe'en. It was the end of the old cycle, the beginning of the new. A time of transition — life, death, new life. A time when the thin veil between the living and dead, the real and the supernatural, was briefly lowered. Ancestors were remembered because, for the Celts, death was merely the halfway stage of a long journey.

It was a time for fires. Fires meant purification and they were lit on the old high places, the hill tops, mounds and tumuli. The old tracks were illuminated, the 'fairy chain' came alive, the magic light reflected in the moats and ponds. The spent forces of autumn were ritually burned away, leaving nothing for the forces of evil to feed upon. Livestock was slaughtered. It was an admission that, at this time, life had to wind down, a low-key existence must be adopted. When November 5th was declared a public holiday the bonfires were moved a few days forward. But in Cheshire's deepest country places the celebration of the fire's purification and protection was kept to the rightful day. On Toot Hill, Macclesfield, the sacred flame was kindled. In Alvanley villagers ran through the bonfires and farmers made Hallowe'en processions around their fields carrying blazing torches. We recall the words of Dom Robert Petit-Pierre on the purification of the leys — a clean-up, a blessing. And all this was happening many centuries after the Celtic civilisation had been broken up — some of it in living memory.

Other traditions were particularly associated with Cheshire. One remained as 'souling,' in which children and adults march from house to house singing traditional songs in exchange for small, spiced 'soul cakes.' Malpas, Frodsham and Halton were great centres for souling. At Northwich and Tarporley the practice had a more obvious link with Celtic ritual with the use of hobby-horses fashioned from horses' skulls with the jawbones hinged so that the teeth could be made to snap alarmingly. At Higher Whitley the skull was ceremoniously buried while villagers conducted a funeral service. The practice of dressing up as animals was one thing that worried the clergy at the time — a rather too obvious sign that pagan ways had not been abandoned. This is probably why such things later turned into pantomime, a joke — not the sort of thing you ought to be seen taking too seriously.

After Samhain came the neutrality of winter. But then, in February, the bleakest time, there was Imbolc, later to be Candlemas, a glimpse of light again. Then there was the choosing of mates in preparation for the spring marriage; what we called earlier the 'cranking up of the seasonal mechanism.' The king and queen are chosen. The earth has been purified and consecrated and placed under the supervision of the goddess — Brigid, the nurse or midwife. The first spark of life begins to flare.

And then it is Maytime. On May Eve, Beltaine, the fire is rekindled, but this time it is more than a purification. It is an awakening. Patience has been exhausted. The people — and the earth — must do what is necessary to ensure a harvest. Washington Irving, passing through Cheshire in the 1820s, caught an idyllic glimpse of the Mayday atmosphere on the banks of the holy river Dee. He wrote:

'I shall never forget the delight I felt on first seeing a Maypole. It was close by the picturesque old bridge that stretches across the river from the quaint little city of Chester. I had already been carried back into the former days by the antiquities of that venerable place. The May-pole on the margin of that poetic stream completed the illusion. My fancy adorned it with wreaths of flowers and peopled the green bank with all the dancing revelry of May-day. The mere sight of this May-pole gave a glow to my feeling and spread a charm over the country for the rest of the day; and, as I traversed a part of the fair plain of Cheshire, and the beautiful borders of Wales and looked from among swelling hills down a long green valley, through which "the Deva wound its wizard stream" my imagination turned it all into a perfect Arcadia.'

The dance around the maypole was an entirely sexual rite, both in symbolism and fact. It was a question of 'making the sap to rise.' And, the sap having risen, the male and female dancers repaired to the woods. The fact that this later became an end in itself doesn't necessarily detract from the force of the ritual. In the north at least the whole May festival was permeated with sexuality both after the maypole dancing and before—when couples would spend the night in the fields and emerge in the dawn to wash their faces in the hill top dew and bring home voluptuously-budding boughs from the woods. It was a joyful explosion, if anything freed from inhibition by its religious aspect. But it didn't last. The Arcadian revelry was already disappearing when Washington Irving passed through Cheshire, to be replaced by the prim spectacle that greeted folklorist Charles Hardwick in the early 1860s. In his *Traditions, Superstitions and Folklore of Lancashire and the North of England* (1872) he wrote:

'A few years ago I attended a May-day gathering at a village in North Cheshire; but the dancers, as well as the May Queen, were all children, and the spectators chiefly ladies and gentlemen from Manchester and its neighbourhood. It was a very pretty sight and was patronised by the neighbouring "squire" and his family, but it lacked the healthy rusticity which I had anticipated from the hearty enjoyment of lusty farm labourers and their sweethearts in the old-fashioned May-day dance.'

It's fairly clear what Hardwick expected the lusty labourers to be doing with their sweethearts. And he was to be even more disappointed in later years, as the festival's decline became more rapid. The Rev. J. E. Sedgewick, of St. Alban's Church, Cheetwood, Manchester, even switched the event to Whit Week to tie in with the city's main holiday. 'The affair was little distinguishable from an ordinary holiday,' recorded Hardwick sadly. 'It certainly lacked the necessary rusticity to suggest any strong sympathy with the rural festival of the "olden time".'

There's a wealth of meaning in the Victorian writer's use of the word 'rusticity.' But what was the original festival of 'olden time'—the one which even preceded the traditional medieval maypole dance? What, in fact, was the maypole for? Tom Graves, the dowser and 'earth acupuncturist,' sees the pole as a wooden needle, serving a similar function to the standing stones placed on their founts of power (in dowsing terms usually a place where underground streams cross, although the streams themselves may be flows of earth-energy rather than orthodox water courses). The energy aroused by the ritual dance has to be primed, Graves says, to work for fertility. And it is conditioned by the suitably-aroused state of mind of the dancers before being distributed to the fields via the point of the still-living wooden needle piercing the receptive earth while attached to the dancers by ribbons of foliage. It's an appealing idea.

And what of the May Queen? Was she also ritually fertilised at the climax of the ceremony centred on sites like the Bridestones? Did she nurture her child through the lazy months of summer, as the earth too prepared to give birth?

VIII
NATURAL MAGIC

DOCTOR John Dee, astrologer, scientist and magician, arrived in Manchester in 1595. He had been appointed warden of Christ's College and he was not wildly excited about it. For a man who had been occult adviser to Elizabeth I, a leading figure in the world of espionage (his code number, curiously enough, was 007) and quite probably a drinking companion of Shakespeare, Manchester must have seemed like the armpit of the universe. The town was already accumulating a hierarchy of hard-nosed businessmen and was seen as a bastion of small-minded provincialism. Dee kept a low profile.

Nevertheless he did apply himself to discovering what there was to be discovered about this northern outpost. He investigated its history and its topography; he had detailed maps made of the area. For when Dee studied a place he went to the roots, looking into legends and ancient customs. The essence of geomancy — the study of earth forces and landscape patterns against a cosmic backcloth — was something he naturally understood. In fact the breadth of knowledge Dee displayed in these matters is itself a pointer to the existence of a hidden tradition in which the secrets of earth magic have been preserved from ancient times.

John Dee was a Welshman. His family came from the northern tip of Radnorshire and he had a vast knowledge of the history, legends and layout of the border area now covered by the counties of Powys, Clwyd, Shropshire and Cheshire. In these areas he researched the secrets of ancient sites. But by the time he came to live in the north he had already made his most notable 'discovery' in Somerset. This was the amazing astrological garden known as the Glastonbury Zodiac, in which celestial symbols were found to be marked out by the shapes of rivers, hills and extensive earthworks over miles of countryside. If you accept the Glastonbury Zodiac exists you have to agree it is the most mind-bending example of prehistoric engineering anywhere in the world. It was rediscovered in 1929 by Mrs. Katherine Maltwood and is now discernible only with the use of large-scale ordnance survey maps and aerial photographs. Dee, who didn't have either, seems to have charted it with unbelievable accuracy. The zodiac 'shews that the ancients understode all which today the learned know to be factes,' he noted. But how did Dee know (a) that it existed and (b) how it was laid out? If you reject any suggestion that the doctor got the information from one of the angelic spirits with whom he and his colleague Edward Kelley had many a meaningful dialogue, it must be assumed that knowledge of the zodiac had been handed down as part of some arcane rural tradition.

If Dee knew about Glastonbury and the zodiac, it would be remarkable if he was not aware of other power centres and the network of ancient sites which connect them. In fact there are strong suggestions that he did. The researches of Dee's biographer Richard Deacon have established that the doctor spent a lot of time 'visiting ancient churches and the sites of ruined castles.' It is suggested that Dee was merely seeking out his own family roots in Wales, but it is difficult to imagine what he would have found in these places, especially in Radnorshire where even in Dee's time virtually all that remained of the castles were green mounds, many of which are enlarged tumuli. Similarly, there is usually more to be learned from the siting of churches in this border area than from the modest buildings. Later, Dee was said to be studying archaeology and 'seeking out ancient camp sites.' The research of the Radnorshire Society has special reference to Dee's 'keen interest' in ancient sites as 'something which has not so far received much attention.' Possibly it has not received attention because it appeared to be a minor sideline of Dee's which had no connection with his main fields of interest.

But Dee was also a dowser, apparently working with the hazel twig and the pendulum. He was much in demand for recovering lost property by means of divination and seems to have investigated many of the stranger properties of the pendulum, later revealed by T. C. Lethbridge, for probing 'other worlds.' Dowsers, said Dee, had the 'supra normal powers not of a magitien but of a peculiar and scientific qualitie.' Indeed, he always denied he was involved with magic, preferring to talk of natural forces. If none of Dee's remaining writings reflect any 'amazing discoverie' of the alignment of ancient sites, it was probably because the archaic system was still relatively well-recognised in the countryside even as late as the sixteenth century. It would certainly not be seen as anywhere near as extraordinary as the Glastonbury Zodiac and there is small-enough mention of that in what has survived of Dee's written notes.

Dee described the terrestrial zodiac as 'Merlin's Secret,' underlining the persistent belief in a connection between the landscape mysteries of Britain and the Arthurian legends. The zodiac (there are several other alleged examples in Britain, including a suggested Wirral Zodiac, for which, unfortunately, no evidence has yet been presented) was seen by Mrs Maltwood as the real source of the 'round table' symbol. Merlin, who traditionally supplied the table, is credited with introducing many other ancient monuments. Long before Dee's time, Geoffrey of Monmouth wrote down as accepted history the story that the stones of Stonehenge were procured by Merlin from Ireland. Throughout Britain you may find standing stones, dolmens, tumuli, hills and caves with names attaching them to Arthur and Merlin. And this is no less true, as we have seen, in the North West, from Alderley Edge to Cumbria.

Dee's antiquarian studies in Cheshire appear to date from around 1574, more than twenty years before he actually moved to Manchester. He is on record as having had discussions with certain scholars at Chester and inquiring into antiquities in the area, proceeding then to the Welsh Marches. And according to Edward Baines 'the learned and venerable Camden' sought the aid of 'that famous mathematician J. Dee, Warden of Manchester College,' during excavations at the Roman (and probably pre-Roman) site at Castlefields, south of the town. This site, once known as Giant's Castle, is the suggested location of Manchester's own Arthurian legend. It was said to be the lair of the giant Tarquin, slain by Lancelot after many others had died in the attempt. The main Roman roads in this part of Britain were believed to converge at Castlefields, now a heavily built-up area. And Alex Sanders, the most famous of modern magicians in Britain, said northern witches had long considered the spot a place of power and sanctity.

It seems that most of the threads of research unwound in this book were at some time gathered together by John Dee. In the eyes of an Elizabethan magician, the study of ancient sites, the art of dowsing, the unearthing of old customs and legends, the link between cosmic and terrestrial forces and the search for the secrets Merlin might have known, were all inextricably interwoven. In his study of what was then called 'natural magic' — defined as 'the force above human reason which is the active principle in Nature' — Dee sensed the existence of a corpus of hidden knowledge which might bring man into a more intimate relationship with his environment.

But Dee also came to the conclusion that this knowledge could not be acquired entirely from academic research. At some stage a spiritual link would have to be forged. It was this realisation that led Dee into the practices which tarnished his reputation as a brilliant scholar and scientist in the eyes of academic historians. Richard Deacon believed that Dee's own aptitude as a dowser convinced him that there were

Dr. John Dee, astrologer, scientist and magician.

certain natural forces with which man could communicate. But what Dee wanted to reach was the *intelligence* behind nature, and he seems to have been uncertain about the wisdom of attempting to combine the detached approach of the scientist with the psychic submission of the 'sensitive.' This led him to take up with Edward Kelley, whose clairvoyant talents were only equalled by his abilities as a con man. Nevertheless, the famous 'angelic conversations,' conducted through Kelley's mediumship under Dee's scientific supervision and long condemned as phoney, have acquired greater credibility in the light of recent theories. Dee and Kelley may not have been in contact with forces as close to God as they imagined, but they certainly seemed to have picked up some kind of wavelength.

Baines talks of when Dee and Kelley 'held correspondencies with the various spirits of the elements on the principles of the Rosicrucian philosophy and affirmed that they could bind to their service and imprison in a ring, a mirror or a stone, some fairy, sylph or salamander.' This has much in common with the 'natural magic' practised by modern witches. The traditional elementals are: sylph (air), salamander (fire), undine (water) and gnome (earth). T. C. Lethbridge related entities of this type to certain forcefields found in the countryside. According to Alex Sanders, conjuring up these so-called spirits really means isolating the elements in your own nature which relate to earth, water, fire or air. By tuning into your earth element—i.e. carrying out a certain meditation exercise designed to bring you in contact with the earth or slow down your 'vibrations' to an earth level—you may actually perceive the spirit representative of the life-force in the earth, the so-called elf or gnome we encountered earlier and which the journalist Paul Screeton says he glimpsed on a ley line. Sanders, quoted in Stewart Farrar's book *What Witches Do,* says of these entities: 'Being so close to man they are occasionally discernible without a deliberate act of projection (as presumably carried out by Dee and Kelley). If you are very quick and smart sometimes in the country you can see them, like a shadow in the corner of your eye.'

Dee approached these matters in much the same way as a parapsychologist might today—working, as far as possible, from an accepted scientific standpoint. Dee worked with Kelley much as the American scientist Dr. Andrija Puharich worked with spoon-bender Uri Geller. And their scientific reputations suffered in the same way. The angelic conversations ruined Dee's reputation as the most brilliant mind of his era. And Puharich's reputation slumped rapidly when he wrote of a continued dialogue between himself, Geller and alleged extra-terrestrial intelligences.

Witches, of course, do not have this problem. They aren't seeking a scientific framework for their beliefs; they have no academic credibility to lose. Even though John Dee came close to being persecuted as a witch, we must assume he never was one. Nevertheless, as an outsider, Dee appears to have gathered considerable information from the rural magical tradition. The fact that he penetrated further than most outsiders is, as Richard Deacon says, probably a tribute to his abilities as a secret agent.

Few notable British magicians—that is, the ones we hear about—have any hereditary basis for their practices. As such, witches would say, they were little more than dabblers. But Alex Sanders is an exception ... an investigative magician with a background in the country cult.

*   *   *   *

As far as the general public is concerned, Alex Sanders is the man who put Alderley Edge back on the magical map. He's the most famous magician to work in Cheshire since an elderly Dee packed his bags and went south to die. Sanders was born in Liverpool, of Welsh descent. He believes one of his ancestors was the Welsh hero Owain Glyndwr, well known for his ability to call spirits from the vasty deep. Witches have long claimed Glyndwr as one of their own, and they claimed Sanders too, at the age of seven, when he was initiated by his granny. Alex became the first male in his family for many generations to have this honour, after catching the old lady performing one of her rituals in the living room. When she died, Sanders, then living in Manchester, lost his family-tie with the craft and had to swot up the academic side of magic, delving into ancient spell books or grimoires from the local library. After some years following the 'left hand path' (black magic) to unearned riches, personal tragedy led him to give up his evil ways and return to a kind of natural magic—in his case an apparently-potent blend of Celtic witchcraft and the more complex ideas favoured by the likes of Eliphas Levi and Aleister Crowley. Before long Alex Sanders had become the new wizard of Alderley.

Sanders and his Cheshire coven made no secret of their use of the Edge. After it became widely known that nude rites were practised there, the hill once again became a place of pilgrimage. Every Hallowe'en the fields were dotted with lights as parties of witch-hunters armed with torches and cameras roamed the Edge looking for the action. Often one patrol would creep up on a group of shadowy figures in some secret hollow only to discover another patrol eating its sandwiches. They never found the witches though. Crafty covens apparently used to change the date of their festival until the fuss died down.

As a hereditary witch, Sanders says he can draw on an ancient wisdom preserved from long before Celtic days. In fact he traces it back to the lost continent of Atlantis. As Chevalier Alexander Sanders, he began in 1961 a society known as the Knights of Deucalion—the Order of the Flood, which, according to its prospectus, 'spends its time gathering information to do with Atlantis and bringing it into practice in the form of ritual which can be used in everyday life.' Members of the Order see the system of power-points as something developed by the advanced minds of Atlantean priests who escaped the doomed continent before it sank beneath the waves. The writer Anthony Roberts, who has developed the theory in his book *Atlantean Traditions in Ancient Britain,* uses it to account for much of traditional folklore—especially stories of strange giants connected with ancient sites, like the aforementioned Tarquin or the rival giants at Stockport and Arden Hall, Cheshire, who threw large stones at each other.

It is on the properties and functions of ancient sites that the two sides of modern witchcraft — simple instinctive, land-based fertility cult and heir to a sophisticated system of knowledge from some forgotten golden age — come together. It has been alleged that the witch cult as it exists today goes back no further than Sanders's predecessor as king witch, the late Gerald Gardner, who was accused of inventing a good many 'ancient rituals.' Certainly the witches we read about as victims of state-persecution over the centuries do not seem to have been strong on organisation.

But there are too many pointers to a tradition of earth-consciousness for the witches' claims to be entirely rejected. Too many echoes of hallowed practices concerned with solar and lunar influence. And in a society governed entirely by the agricultural cycle, dependent for survival on the goodwill of the earth and emotionally dependent on the strict observance of essentially Celtic festivals, it is not unreasonable to expect that there have been a few people, since Druidic days, who knew what they were doing.

Mrs. Joan Rogers says there are now more than two thousand people in Cheshire and Lancashire who have been 'presented to the goddess.' These, she says, are not the people who have turned to paganism to fulfil some inner demand or the need to belong to a secret cult, but those who were raised in the 'old ways' by their families. If this seems like a remarkable number of hereditary witches, Mrs. Rogers has another surprise. There are, she claims, fewer today than there were one hundred years ago, despite a fashionable swing to nature-mysticism.

Although unused to the terminology of the ley-hunters and their kind, these people say they have always been aware of centres of terrestrial energy. They knew the plain of Cheshire and the sanctuaries in the hills just as the aborigines knew and followed the tracks of their gods in Australia's arid wastes. But their vision of life was the misty, pastel-coloured vision of the Celt. Their ancestors knew no certainties, only possibilities, and existence was a delicately-orchestrated symphony of alternating currents. Sometimes it was pastoral, sometimes harsh and strident, but there was a basis for harmony and it rested on a workable relationship with the elements. When Christianity arrived, the Celts allowed it to mingle with the old ways and it was not incompatible because it dealt more with human relations than the alliance of man and nature in an agricultural framework. It was accepted fairly easily, because the Celts didn't see things in black and white, didn't deal in absolutes. And in an age when uncertainties are bounding back, the Celtic viewpoint has a new appeal.

Witchcraft, Mrs. Rogers maintains, is psychologically geared to the British temperament. It is a method of development which is essentially gentler that some of the Eastern disciplines now flooding the West. The difference, Mrs. Rogers says, is that the Eastern systems demand you destroy your old way of life before you can switch to a new one — undergo a kind of death before you can learn to live correctly. Witchcraft is said to allow you to adapt slowly to the 'cosmic viewpoint,' attuning your rhythm to nature's without the risk of a nervous breakdown. 'It's like a greedy child at a party, compared to a good-mannered child,' she explains. 'A witch is trained to eat slowly, to eat only a little and to appreciate it. You have got to be incredibly patient.'

She refers to Alan Garner's Alderley experience, described in Chapter II, in which 'a kaleidoscope of images expanded so quickly that they fragmented . . . too many, too fast for individual detail or remembrance.' An example of psychic overload, she says. Someone trained in the 'old ways' would have been able to slow down the experience, savour the details and learn from it. But it is this kind of experience that prompts people to look further. Garner has since investigated Cheshire leys for himself and believes his home at Goostrey, near Jodrell Bank, is on the site of a Bronze Age henge.

We don't know what experiences Dr. Dee had during his travels around the ancient sites, but Mrs. Rogers says local witches, who are interested in Dee's work, are convinced he consulted the witches of the day—the hereditary guardians of the earth culture—to get the raw material for his 'scientific' research. It would be naive to assume that witchcraft, whether you regard it as a genuine religion or merely the application of rural common-sense, has all the answers. But at least it doesn't dodge the questions.

Appendix i
Small, Dark and Dangerous . . .

IN the Dark Ages, when the Celtic and Roman civilisations had broken down, there remained, in the area around the Bridestones, an ancient race which guarded its secrets with some savagery. According to a paper published by the Lancashire and Cheshire Historical Society in the 1880s, these people were neither Saxon nor Briton, but a throw-back to a much earlier race. People had a saying: 'There are English-men, Frenchmen and Biddlemoor men.' They were dark-skinned, long-skulled and heavy-browed and are said to have survived into the nine-teenth century. S. G. Wildman described them as having a bad reputa-tion for secretiveness, criminal activities and their habit of going ber-serk in fights. They would 'lead you into the trackless bog and watch you drown.'

Appendix ii
Tuning In

EDNA, the Manchester dowser and psychometrist, says anyone can learn to work with the divining rod or pendulum. These are merely aids to awakening the ability and eventually may even be discarded. Edna works with her hands and says she can pick up images in her mind from handling small stones — and pick up vibrations with her feet, 'which is why water diviners are supposed to take their shoes off.'

Edna agrees with T. C. Lethbridge that it is not only water, metals and stone which emit and transmit vibrations which dowsers can sense. Walking through the woods at Alderley, she says, she can pick up emanations of the life-force in the trees. 'I was checking the magnetic fields of trees at Alderley and, with one beautiful old tree with a very wide bole, it was so strong that I had to step back a considerable dist-ance to check the reaction with my hands.' Suggestions that particular trees are strongly attracted to the 'geodetic force' on alignments of ancient sites were explored by the late Guy Underwood, a pioneer ley-dowser, in his book *The Pattern of the Past*.

Those interested in trying to pick up power from megalithic monu-ments are advised by the Welsh dowser John Williams to relax, still all thoughts, place the hands, palms flat against the stone a little more than half way up and be prepared to wait. Mr. Williams believes the force may once have been used to some extent as a system of communication — with primitive messages passed from stone to stone. Many dowsers have become convinced from personal experience that the force flows in straight lines, but Watkins' ley-system is not strict enough for Mr. Williams, who tests alignments against what he calls the SCEMB system. The letters stand for the only features he is prepared to accept as proof of a ley — stones, cairns or camps, earthworks, mounds and barrows. Even so, he says, he has charted convincing alignments on every single one-inch OS map of the British Isles . . . checking out more than four thousand ancient sites. The power, he believes, is manifested on several 'wavelengths.' The Fifth Wavelength is the one most often experienced by dowsers at megalithic sites. It hits the dowser like an electric shock, sometimes bouncing him away from the stone. Some people experience it at once; in others the ability may be developed, the effects becoming more intense with practice. Like Edna, he says: don't give up if it doesn't happen at once. Finally, for those who favour a more mystical approach, Mrs. Rogers has this advice: 'If you go to a charged spot and want to be charged yourself (with physical or psychic energy) you should ask in a proper manner. Ask the Goddess for help and just sit quietly.'

But if your purpose in seeking power is less than pure, watch out . . . 'these spots have a way of bouncing it back at people when they want to put it to bad use.'

Bibliography

Joan Alcock: *Discovering Cheshire* (Shire).

Edward Baines: *History of Lancashire.*

Janet and Colin Bord: *Mysterious Britain. The Secret Country* (Paladin).

C. A. Burland: *Echoes of Magic* (Peter Davies).

Michael Dames: *The Avebury Cycle* (Thames and Hudson).

Richard Deacon: *John Dee* (Muller).

Stewart Farrar: *What Witches Do* (Sphere and Peter Davies).

Dion Fortune: *Avalon of the Heart* (Aquarian). *The Goatfoot God* (Aquarian and Star paperback).

Alan Garner: *The Wierdstone of Brisingamen. Red Shift* (Lion).

Gerald Gardner: *Witchcraft Today.*

Tom Graves: *Needles of Stone* (Turnstone).

Charles Hardwick: *Traditions, Superstitions and Folklore of Lancashire and the North West.*

Francis Hitching: *Earth Magic* (Picador). *Pendulum* (Fontana).

Christina Hole: *Traditions and Customs of Cheshire.*

June Johns: *King of the Witches* (Pan).

T. C. Lethbridge: *Ghost and Ghoul. Ghost and Divining Rod. The Legend of the Sons of God* (Routledge and Kegan Paul).

John Michell: *The View Over Atlantis* (Abacus).

Guy Ragland Phillips: *Brigantia* (Routledge and Kegan Paul).

E. and M. A. Radford (Ed. C. Hole): *The Encyclopedia of Superstitions* (Hutchinson).

Readers Digest: *Folklore, Myths and Legends of Britain.*

Alwyn and Brinley Rees: *Celtic Heritage* (Thames and Hudson).

Alfred Rimmer: *Ancient Stone Crosses of England* (Garnstone Press).

Anthony Roberts: *Atlantean Traditions in Ancient Britain* (Rider).

Anne Ross: *Pagan Celtic Britain* (Routledge).

Ward Rutherford: *The Druids and Their Heritage* (Gordon and Cremonesi).

Paul Screeton: *Quicksilver Heritage* (Abacus).

Jacqueline Simpson: *The Folklore of the Welsh Border* (Batsford).

Guy Underwood: *The Pattern of the Past* (Abacus).

W. J. Varley: *Cheshire Before the Romans* (Chester Community Council).

Alfred Watkins: *The Old Straight Track* (Abacus).

S. G. Wildman: *The Black Horsemen—English Inns and King Arthur* (Garnstone).

Colin Wilson: *The Occult* (Mayflower paperback). *Mysteries* (Hodder and Stoughton).

Dudley Wright: *Druidism* (E.P.).